Forgive Me,
I Meant to Do It

Also by Gail Carson Levine

Dave at Night

Ella Enchanted

Ever

Fairest

A Tale of Two Castles

The Two Princesses of Bamarre

The Wish

—

THE PRINCESS TALES

The Fairy's Return and Other Princess Tales (Collection)

The Fairy's Mistake

The Princess Test

Princess Sonora and the Long Sleep

Cinderellis and the Glass Hill

For Biddle's Sake

The Fairy's Return

—

Betsy Red Hoodie

Betsy Who Cried Wolf

Fairy Dust and the Quest for the Egg

Fairy Haven and the Quest for the Wand

Fairies and the Quest for Never Land

Writing Magic: Creating Stories That Fly

False Apology Poems by

Gail Carson Levine

Illustrated by

Matthew Cordell

HARPER
An Imprint of HarperCollins*Publishers*

For information address HarperCollins Children's Books, a division of HarperCollins Publishers,
10 East 53rd Street, New York, NY 10022.
www.harpercollinschildrens.com

Library of Congress Cataloging-in-Publication Data
Levine, Gail Carson.
Forgive me, I meant to do it : false apology poems / by Gail Carson Levine ; illustrated by Matthew Cordell. — 1st ed.
p. cm.
ISBN 978-0-06-178725-6 (trade bdg.)
ISBN 978-0-06-178726-3 (lib. bdg.)
1. Children's poetry, American. 2. Humorous poetry, American. I. Title.
PS3562.E8965T47 2012 2009023978
811'.54—dc22 CIP
AC

Typography by Martha Rago
12 13 14 15 16 LP/RRDC 10 9 8 7 6 5 4 3 2 1
❖
First Edition

To Susan Campbell Bartoletti,
who led me down the poetry path

Acknowledgments

To my poetry teachers, who may deny any connection to me and this book—Kathleen Driskell, Molly Fisk, Sally Keith, Molly Peacock, Vivian Shipley, and Nancy Willard

Contents

This Is Just to Say

My bulldozer
has flattened
the thorny
hedge

which
you mistakenly
expected to sleep behind
until the prince came

Forgive me
I'm charging tourists
ten dollars
to visit the castle

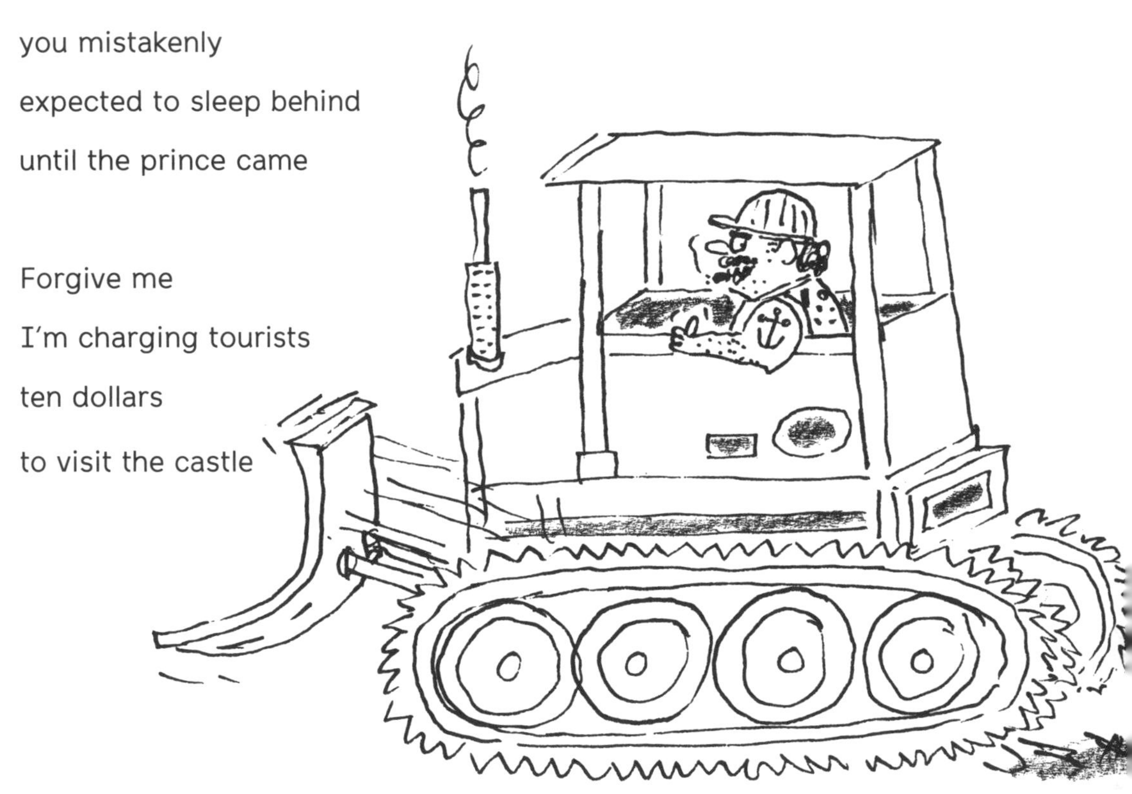

This Is Just to Say

While you were buying
doll dresses
I sanded off
your Barbie's face

which
you constantly
patted
and praised

Forgive me
her beauty
was only
skin deep

This Is Just to Say

Dwarves
you snore
pick your noses
never take a bath

although
I always
encourage you
to be at your best

Forgive me
I'm making myself ugly
and leaving
with the witch

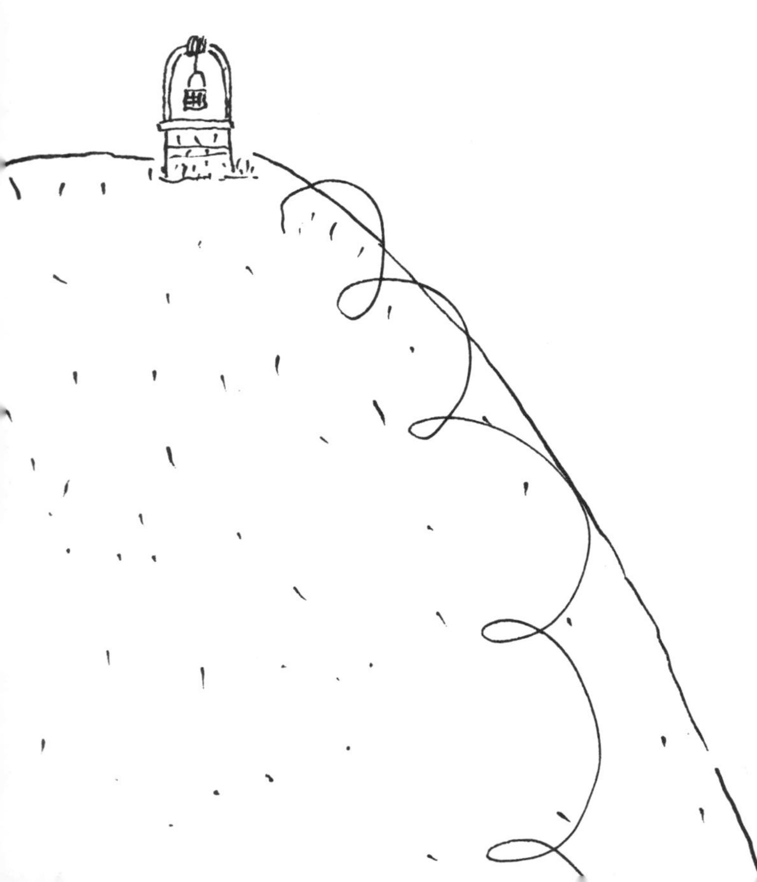

This Is Just to Say

You fell
and cracked
your skull
on the hill

where
I had carefully
placed
a banana peel

Forgive me
Jill
is now
my girlfriend

This Is Just to Say

If you have feet
I hope
you put on
slippers

when
my spaceship thunderously
shattered
your bedroom window

Forgive me
glass
is unknown
on my home planet

Introduction

This Is Just to Say

Instead of at the beginning
I slipped
this introduction
in here

where
my editor excruciatingly loudly
screeched
it does not belong

Forgive me
I also shredded
her red pencil and stirred
the splinters into her tea

Blame my poems on the American poet William Carlos Williams,

who lived from 1883 to 1963 and was a doctor as well as a poet.

Here's his false apology poem:

This Is Just to Say

I have eaten

the plums

that were in

the icebox

and which

you were probably

saving

for breakfast

Forgive me

they were delicious

so sweet

and so cold

—William Carlos Williams

Imagine **his** wife coming downstairs in the morning after dreaming about those plums all night and waking up tasting them. Possibly she opens the icebox door (no refrigerators then) and finds a poem in the neatly washed-and-dried plum bowl. Maybe she laughs or maybe she goes for a very long walk or maybe she eats *his* breakfast and then writes her own false apology poem—

Which you can do too. Many poets have written them, following the form invented by William Carlos Williams. But don't even consider writing this kind of poem unless you can get yourself into a grouchy mood. You will be wasting your time.

If you do decide to write, your poems should be mean, or what's the point? Mine are, and William Carlos Williams's is too, in its subtle way. He's glad he got to those plums first!

You don't need a title, because William Carlos Williams has given you one, which can be repeated endlessly until your reader is completely sick of it. You also don't need a new ninth line, because that's always the same too: *Forgive me.* Notice that there are three stanzas, which you may agree are quite enough, and each stanza is four lines long, which you may think are four too many. The first stanza states the horrible offense. The second stanza describes the effect of the offense. The last stanza begins with "Forgive me" and continues with the false apology, because the writer is not sorry at all. There is no punctuation (how nice!), and the beginning words of only the first and ninth lines need to be capitalized. The line beginnings and endings substitute for capital letters and punctuation. Normally, capitals and punctuation help the reader understand, so be careful to end your lines in a way that is very clear, unless you want to confuse your reader, which might be the wisest course.

Also, think about the rhythm of the lines. After you've cleared everyone out of the house, read your stanzas aloud to help you decide where to end a line. Funny poems are still poems.

You don't have to follow William Carlos Williams's form exactly if you don't want to. I haven't. You can add or subtract lines and stanzas. Or you can abandon the form completely and write false apology poems in your own cruel way.

For those of you who lack an ounce of mean and are reading this book only for research into the psychology of unpleasant people, you can write a real apology poem. However, even this will not be possible if you are too angelic to have anything to apologize for.

Whatever way you do it, have fun and save your poems!

—Gail Carson Levine

This Is Just to Say

I have eaten

your hot fudge

sundae

and the cherry on top

which

I thoughtfully

replaced

with anchovies

Forgive me

I gave three spoonfuls

of ice cream

to the cat

This Is Just to Say

I baked
a cottage
made all
of gingerbread

which
you and your sister
will be unable
to resist

Forgive me
I am hungry
and I prefer my food
young

This Is Just to Say

Tonight

we are eating

dinner

at Aunt Mildred's house

although

you will likely

throw up

when we get home

Forgive me

she made

her peppermint-spinach pudding

just for you

This Is Just to Say

I have chewed
through
the tall
beanstalk

which
you recently
stepped off
way up there

Forgive me
I think
I'm worth
more than five magic beans

This Is Just to Say

In your new prom dress

I danced

all night

with your boyfriend

who

accidentally

spilled grape juice

on the skirt

Forgive me

the stain

is almost

too small to see

This Is Just to Say

I convinced
Cupid
to pair you
with a warthog

whom
you will eternally
cherish
and love

Forgive me
warthogs
are very
affectionate

This Is Just to Say

The sharp teeth

the fur all over your face

and your new tail

are family traits

which

are charmingly

displayed in the portraits

hanging in the den

Forgive us

we should have

told you

sooner

This Is Just to Say

A single rose
adorned the table
while I breakfasted
on your daughter

which
proves regrettably
that I am
just a beast

Forgive me
please send
her sisters
by the next coach

URP

This Is Just to Say

I recieved

my Joon

report

card

which

says I'm definitly

gonna be left

way back

Forgive me

the kids

in my new class

ain't been born yet

This Is Just to Say

I found

an old lamp

and called forth

a genie

who

is busily

granting

my wishes

Forgive me

time-out and *grounded*

and other unpleasant phrases

can no longer be uttered

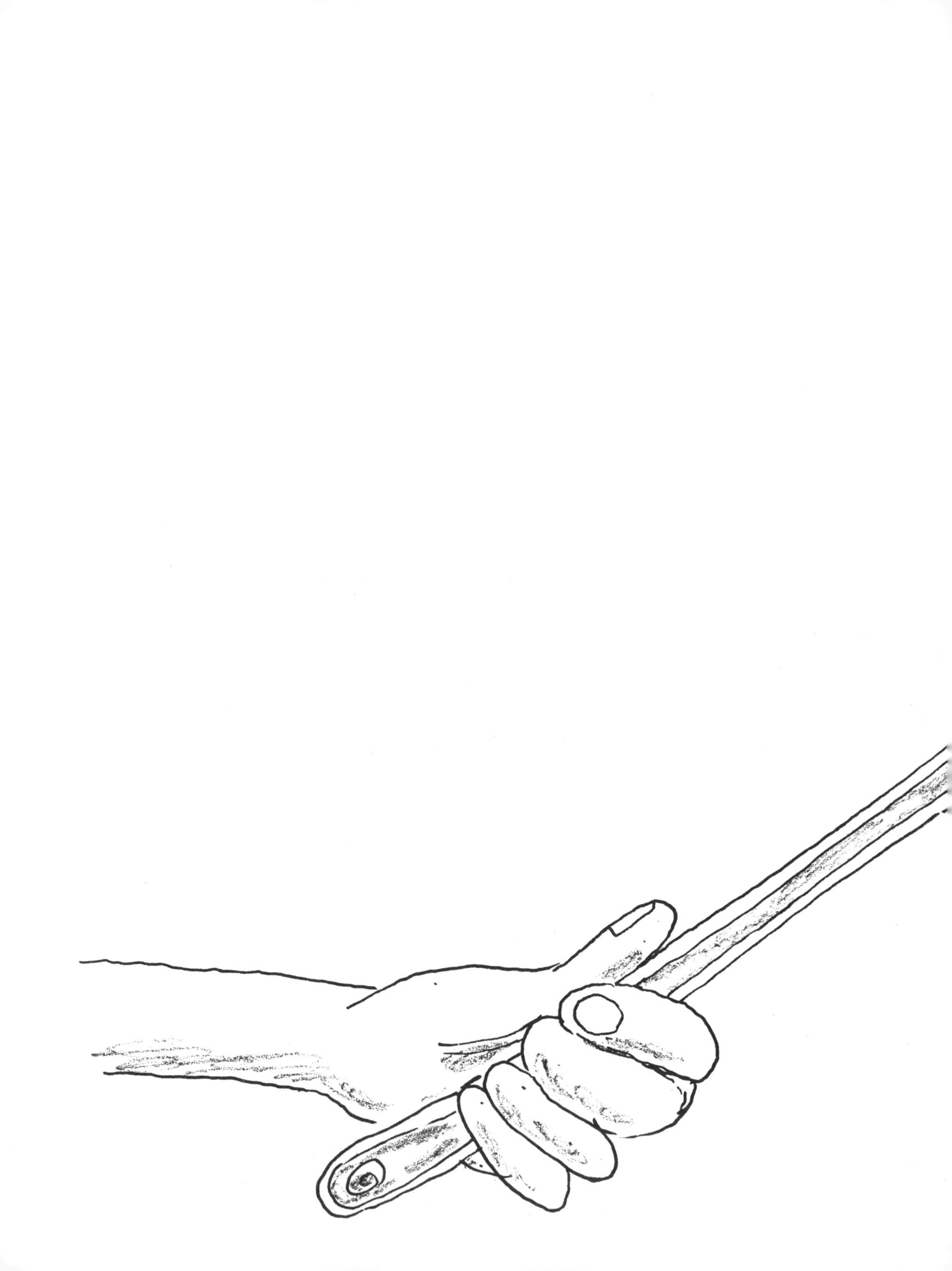

This Is Just to Say

I have cast
a magic spell
on Louie
the bully

which
will soon
turn him
into a fly

Forgive me
my fly swatter
is already
ready

This Is Just to Say

I swiped

your lucky

baseball

cap

which

made you tragically

lose

the state playoff

Forgive me

the cap

keeps the sun

out of my eyes

This Is Just to Say

Spreading
across your skin
is an itchy
blistery rash

which
was deliberately
caused by yours truly
planting poison ivy on your lawn

Forgive me
next time
pay me
for mowing

This Is Just to Say

Ahead of you
you should see
a track
switch

which
will certainly
startle
and confuse you

Forgive me
you think
you can
but you can't

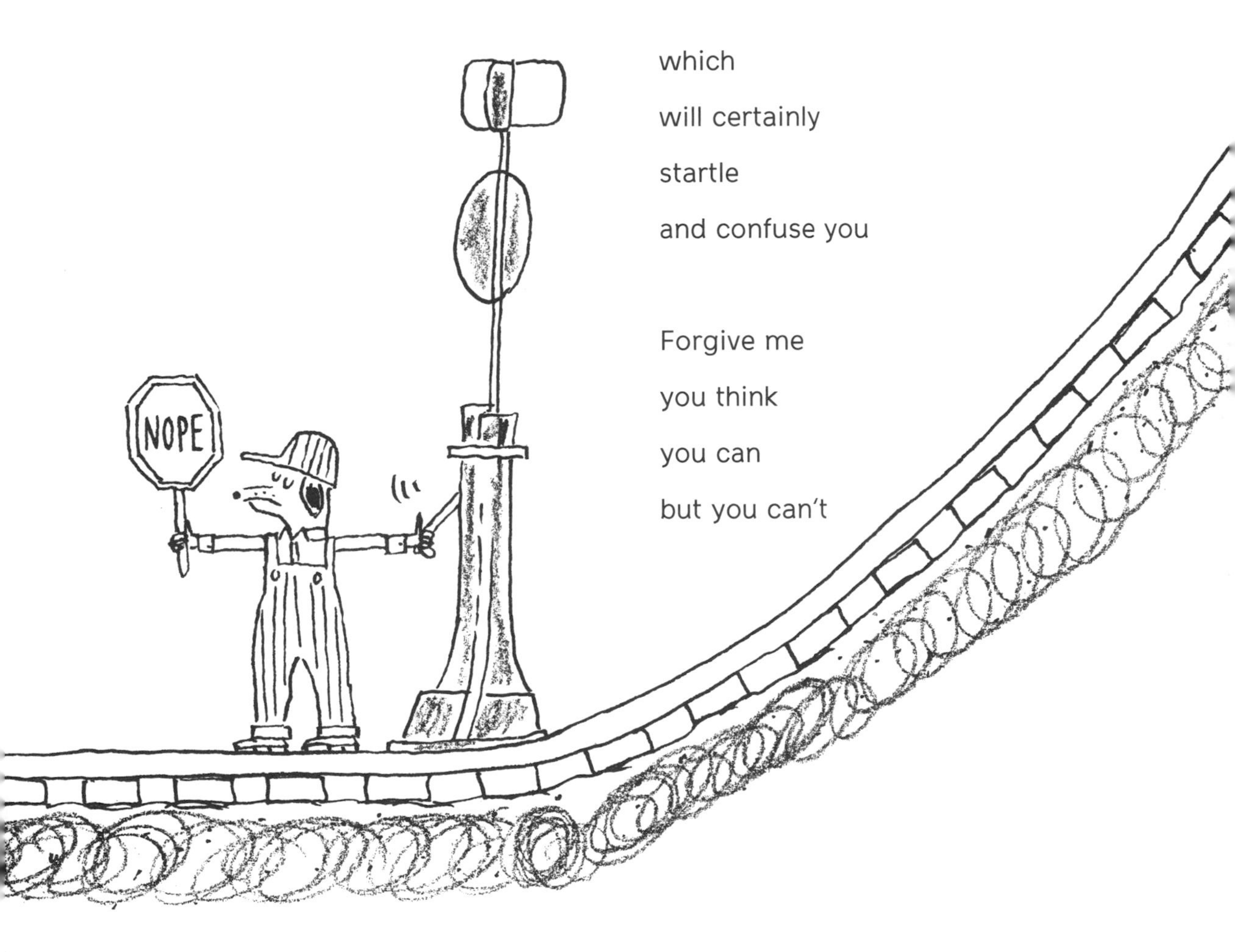

This Is Just to Say

I have shortened
my nose
with your saw

because
honestly
telling lies
is so much fun

Forgive me
I don't care
about becoming
a real boy

This Is Just to Say

You may be jumping around

and skipping

pages

in this book

which

I actually

spent ten years

arranging

Forgive me

I put the curse of the mummy

on anyone

who reads out of order

This Is Just to Say

To get my crimes
off my chest
I broke
into the cemetery

where
I confessed
to the bones
and the tombstones

Forgive me
dead men
tell
no tales

This Is Just to Say

I moved recently
into my new
old
house

through which
you ghoulishly
expected to stump forever
headless and trailing blood

Forgive me
residents
must clean up
after themselves

This Is Just to Say

I have run away

from home

with Muffie

and

they surprisingly

let her

on the plane

Forgive me

we just

landed in—

never mind

This Is Just to Say

They sing
The bear
went over
the mountain

which
leads him repeatedly
to see
other mountains

Forgive me
no one sings the ending
the landslide
and the dead bear

GRANDMA'S
GRUMMBLE
GRUUMBLLE
GRRUMBLLE

This Is Just to Say

When you arrive

I will not be

lying

in my bed

where

you hungrily

hoped

to find me

Forgive me

tell my granddaughter

better one of us

should live

This Is Just to Say

I heard

screams

coming from the cottage

which

I should valiantly

and immediately

have entered

Forgive me

at the time

I preferred

to finish my bubble bath

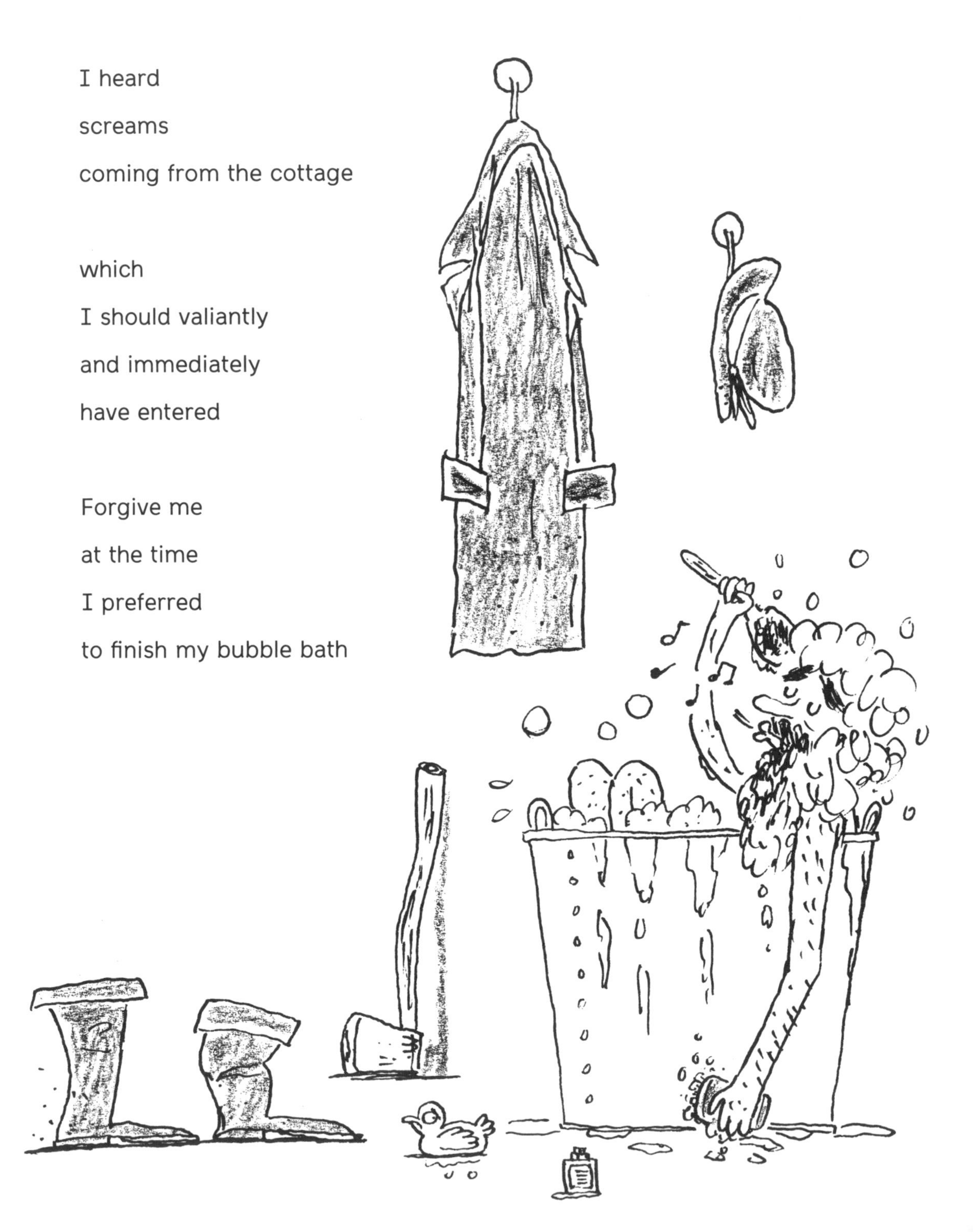

ICK! ACK!
GRANDMA'S
URK!
OWK!
EEEEEK!

This Is Just to Say

I'm the one
who stuck
the cradle
in the tree

which
was probably
a stupid place
to put a baby

Forgive me
I thought
that bough would break
sooner or later

This Is Just to Say

Last night

I plucked

your baby

from your arms

when

you carelessly

fell

asleep

Forgive me

just guess my assumed name

in the Dwarf

Witness Protection Program

This Is Just to Say

I have sent
a hungry lion
into your parents'
hotel room

just when
they were tenderly
talking about
how wonderful you are

Forgive me
I am
starting
an orphanage

This Is Just to Say

I confess
I sliced off
their skinny
tails

which
they seemed awfully
fond
of waving

Forgive me
I wanted symmetry
sightless in front
tailless behind

This Is Just to Say

I, Rapunzel,
and not the witch
have lopped off
my braid

which
you daily
climbed
to me

Forgive me
you’re not worth
the pain
in my scalp

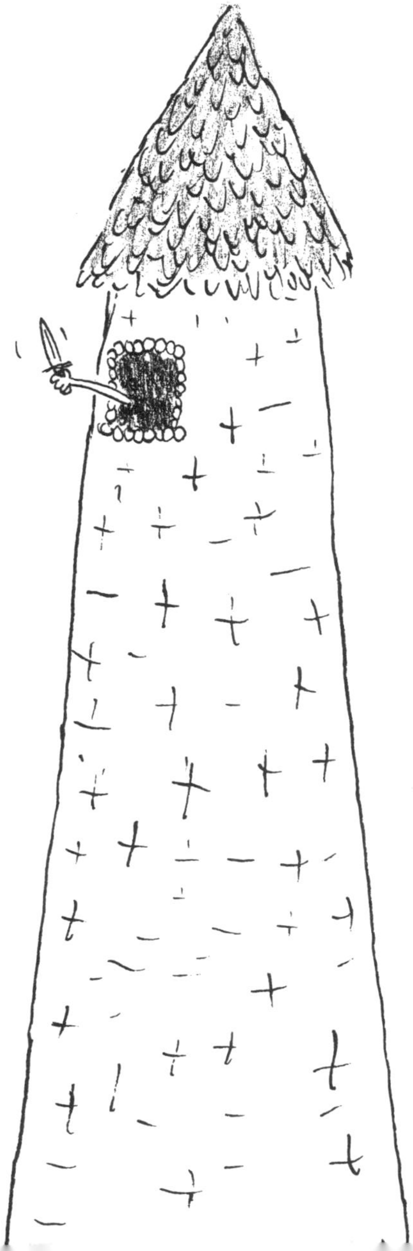

This Is Just to Say

You screamed
while I
yanked out
your hook

which
would doubtlessly
have injured the crocodile
when it ate you

Forgive me
I hate
cruelty
to animals

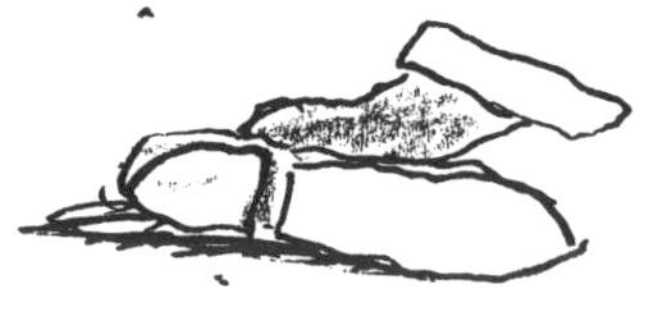

This Is Just to Say

Soon
you will
visit
your cousins

who thoughtlessly
broke your bicycle
and chewed your gum
last time

Forgive me
you're
staying
a month

PHWEET!

This Is Just to Say

It was I

who shoved

you

off the wall

which

you had precariously

perched on

for centuries

Forgive me

all the king's horses

and all the king's men

were bored

This Is Just to Say

By feeling inside
your right snow boot
I located
your diary

which
you moronically
left
where anyone could find it

Forgive me
a year's allowance
and your college fund
will buy my silence

Dear diary,
Can you believe it? Billy actually looked at me today! I could just DIE!!!
$
¢

This Is Just to Say

The principal
may mention
my science project
in a phone call

which
could conceivably
threaten expulsion
and marks on my permanent record

Forgive me
I proved my hypothesis
blood is thicker
than water

This Is Just to Say

I gagged
your little brother
and tied him up
at school

after
you clearly
said what a brat
he is

Forgive me
I can't remember
which locker
I stuffed him in

This Is Just to Say

I have torn
down
the water
spout

which
you obsessively
wanted to climb up
and slide off forever

Forgive me
kick your habit
spin a web
catch a bug

This Is Just to Say

From one cup of organic tomatoes

one tarantula

and two tablespoons of ants

I cooked a stew

which

you gluttonously

devoured

then licked the bowl

Forgive me

you are

what

you eat

This Is Just to Say

I pushed
your boat
out of the gentle
stream

where
you were merrily
singing
and rowing

Forgive me
life
is but
a nightmare

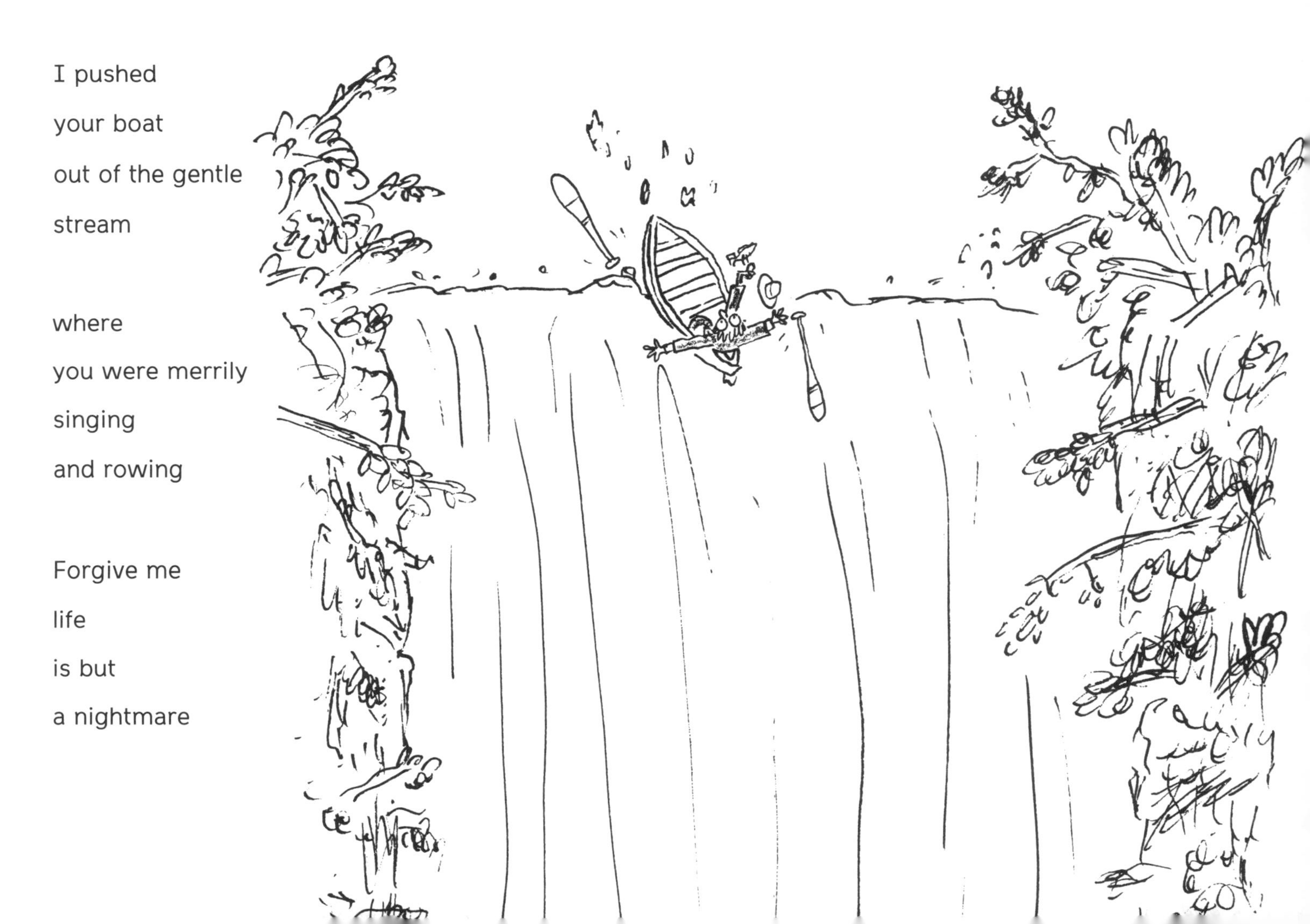

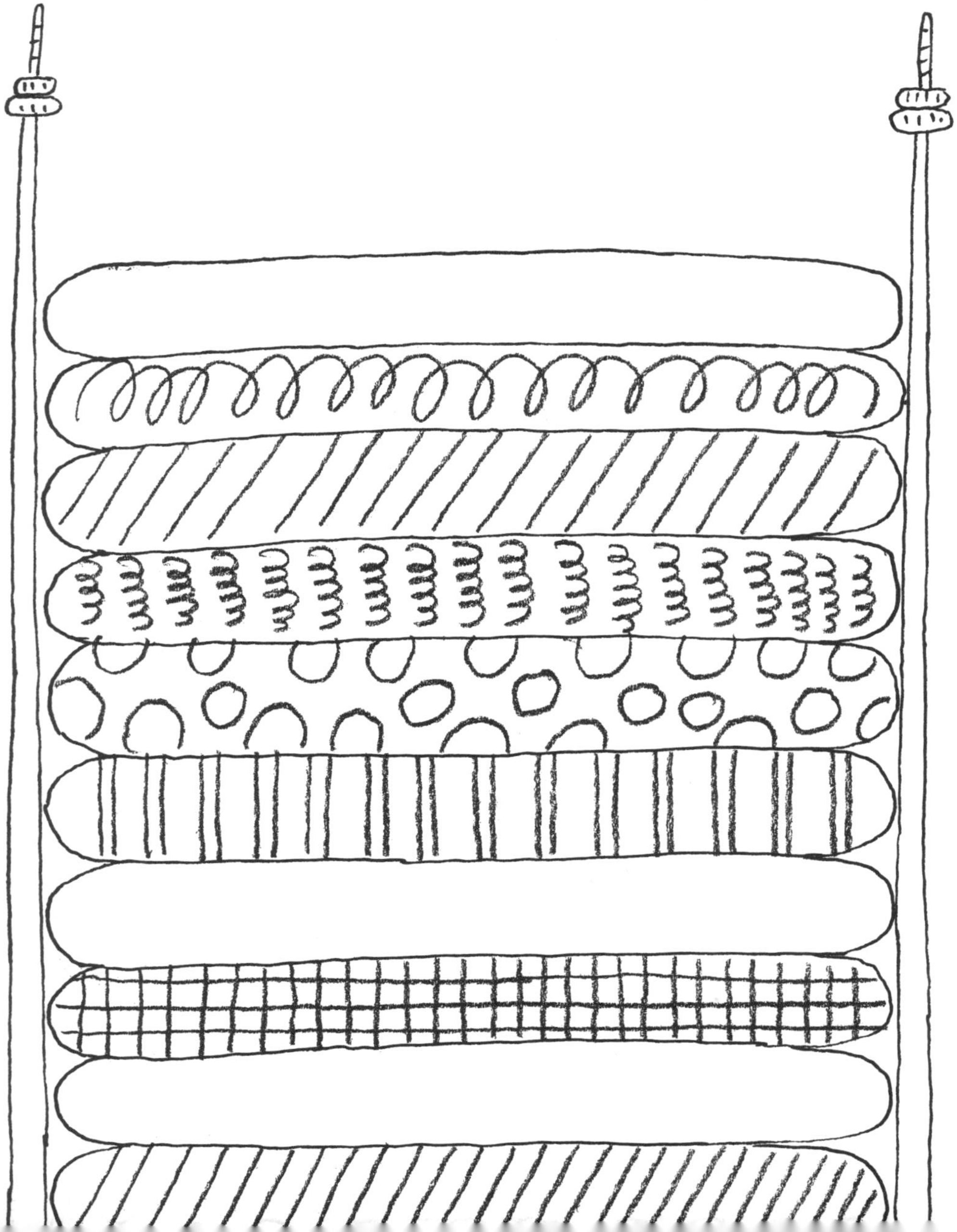

This Is Just to Say

I already knew
the pea
was under
the mattresses

which
helped immeasurably
in faking
the true princess test

Forgive me
I am a true
evil
enchantress

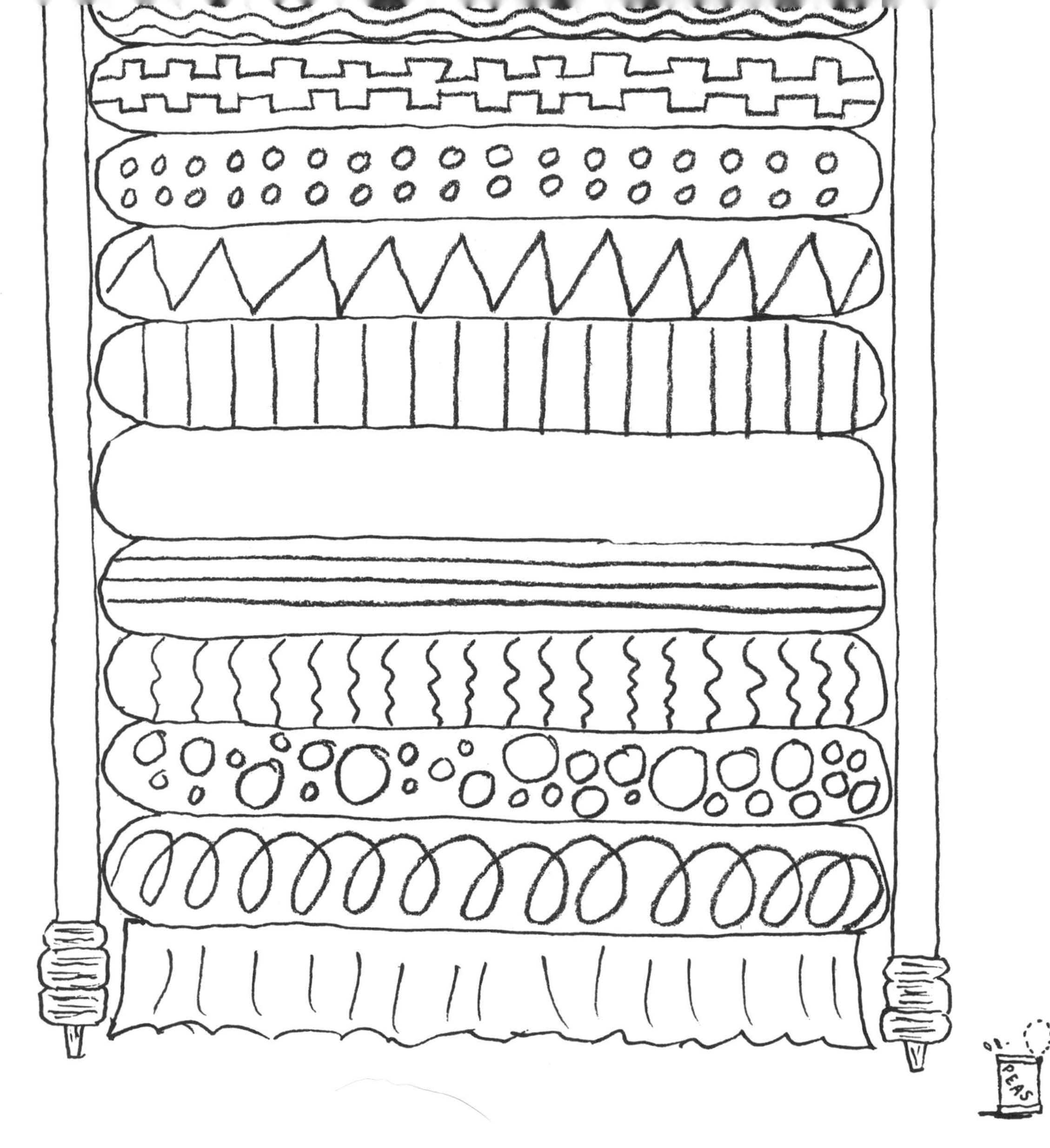
PEAS

This Is Just to Say

The moment
it fell off
I snatched
the glass slipper

which
would gloriously
have led you
to Cinderella

Forgive me
I am one-legged
was shoeless
size 3½

This Is Just to Say

I have found
seventeen
cavities
in your teeth

which
you sincerely
wish
were not there

Forgive me
my drill is ready
and I
am in a bad mood

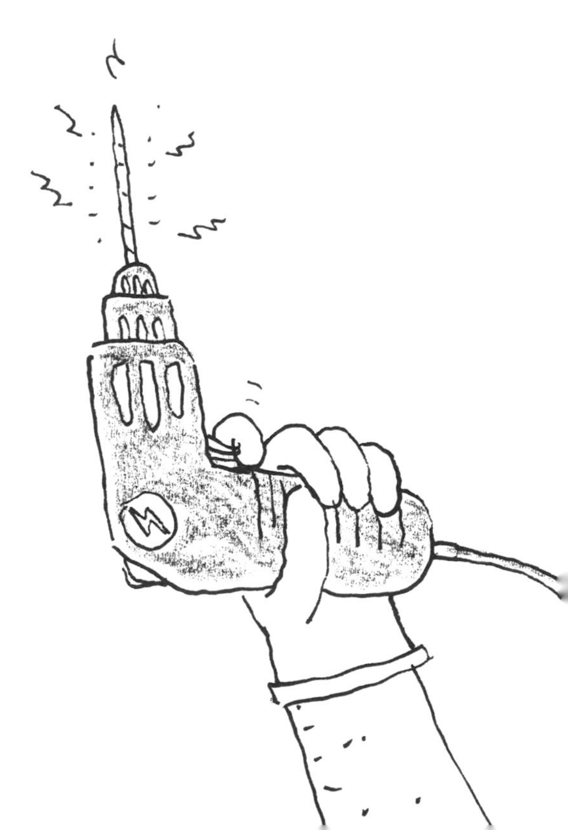

This Is Just to Say

You have reached
the last
of these poems

although
you likely
preferred strep throat
to reading them

Forgive me
I wrote
every one
especially for you